DO IT YOURSELF ONLINE VENTURE

"Unleashing the potential of the top five profitable online businesses"

EmpowerElevates

Dedicated to the reader.

In acknowledgment of the collective spirit, resilience, and boundless potential inherent within every individual.

May this book serve as a source of inspiration and empowerment, propelling you to pursue your aspirations, embrace your passions, and unlock the wealth of possibilities that await on your distinctive journey.

With aspirations for empowerment and elevation.

Acknowledgments

The development of this book has been a
collaborative endeavor.

To those who have joined in this literary exploration,
your unwavering curiosity, active engagement, and
continuous support serve as the pulsating life force
behind these pages. The existence of this work is a
direct result of the dynamic community of readers
who have seamlessly integrated it into their journey of
exploration and learning.

This book stands as a testament to the symbiotic
relationship between authors and readers—an
affirmation of the profound impact that shared
knowledge can have and the boundless possibilities
that arise when words resonate with receptive minds.

With sincere appreciation.

Authors Note

Dear Readers,

As you embark on the pages of this book, I want to
extend my heartfelt gratitude for joining me on this
journey. Your presence and curiosity are the heartbeat
of these words.

This book is more than just a collection of ideas; it's a
shared exploration, a dialogue between the writer and
the reader. I hope that within these pages, you find
inspiration, insights, and perhaps a spark that ignites
your own creative journey.

Writing is a collaborative act, and each reader brings a
unique perspective, adding depth to the narrative. As
you navigate through the chapters, consider this book
as an invitation—to learn, to question, and to embark
on your own path of discovery.

Thank you for being a part of this shared endeavor.
Your engagement is not just appreciated; it is the
essence that breathes life into these words.

Wishing you a rewarding and enriching reading
experience.

Disclaimer

The information provided in this book is for general informational purposes only. The author and publisher make no representation or warranties of any kind, express or implied, about the completeness, accuracy, reliability, or suitability of the information contained herein.

Any reliance you place on such information is strictly at your own risk. The author and publisher will not be liable for any losses or damages arising from the use of this book.

This book is not a substitute for professional advice. Readers are encouraged to seek professional advice or services when needed. The author and publisher disclaim any responsibility for any liability, loss, or risk, personal or otherwise, which is incurred as a consequence, directly or indirectly, of the use and application of any of the contents of this book. All product names, logos, and brands are property of their respective owners. The mention of specific companies or products does not imply endorsement or recommendation.

The views expressed in this book are those of the author and do not necessarily reflect the views of the publisher.

Introduction

"Unveiling the Landscape of Possibility"

Welcome to the exploration of a world where ideas transform into action, and dreams evolve into realities. As we embark on this journey together, I invite you to dive into the landscape of possibility that the digital realm unfolds.

In these pages, we'll unravel the tapestry of DIY online businesses—each chapter is a portal to a different avenue of opportunity.

Whether you're seeking the global reach of e-commerce, the creative expanse of blogging, the freedom of freelancing, the knowledge-sharing in digital courses, or the passive income potential of affiliate marketing, this book is your guide.

But beyond the practical strategies and insights lies a deeper invitation. This is a journey of empowerment, an exploration of the untapped potential within each reader. It's a reminder that the digital landscape is not just a canvas for commerce; it's a space where your unique vision and passion can find expression.

As we embark on this odyssey, let curiosity be our compass, and innovation be our guide. Together, let's uncover the myriad possibilities that await in the world of DIY online businesses.

Here's to the adventure that lies ahead!

Introduction

"The Power of Online Entrepreneurship"

In the vast landscape of the internet, opportunities bloom like digital flowers, waiting to be plucked by those with the vision to see and the will to seize.

In this interconnected age, where the click of a button can transcend borders and time zones, the power of online entrepreneurship has emerged as a formidable force, reshaping economies and empowering individuals in unprecedented ways.

As we stand at the crossroads of the physical and the virtual, it's crucial to recognize the transformative potential that the online business realm holds.

The barriers to entry have crumbled, and the playing field has been leveled. From the bustling streets of metropolises to the quiet corners of remote villages, anyone armed with an idea, a laptop, and an internet connection can embark on a journey of economic self-determination.

This book aims to be a beacon for those who dare to dream beyond the confines of traditional employment, beckoning them into the realm of Do-It-Yourself (DIY) online businesses.

More than a mere handbook, it is a roadmap through the digital landscape, highlighting the signposts that lead to substantial income streams and financial independence.

Setting the Stage:

In the chapters that follow, we will delve into the nuances of online entrepreneurship, exploring not just the 'how' but the 'why' behind the decision to forge one's path in the digital domain.

It is a space where creativity meets commerce, where passion intertwines with profit, and where the bold are rewarded for navigating the uncharted. The stage is set for a transformative journey—one that transcends the conventional boundaries of business guides.

This is not just about creating websites or mastering social media algorithms; it is a narrative of liberation, a tale of individuals emancipating themselves from the shackles of the nine-to-five grind.

Prepare to uncover the secrets of success in online entrepreneurship, where innovation, resilience, and adaptability are the currencies that truly matter. As we navigate the intricacies of this dynamic landscape, remember: the power to shape your destiny lies at the intersection of your ambition and the boundless possibilities of the online world.

Welcome to the adventure of a lifetime.

CHAPTER 1

"E-Commerce Empires Building Your Online Store"

In the vast digital expanse, where possibilities are as limitless as the pixels on a screen, the allure of e-commerce stands out as a beacon for aspiring entrepreneurs.

This chapter embarks on a journey through the dynamic realm of online retail, where the convergence of technology and commerce has given rise to virtual marketplaces that transcend geographical constraints and redefine the very nature of buying and selling.

The Rise of E-Commerce:

The tale begins with the meteoric rise of e-commerce—an ascent propelled by the fusion of consumer demand, technological innovation, and a global shift towards digital connectivity.

Over the past decade, we have witnessed the transformation of shopping from a physical pursuit to a virtual expedition, with online sales soaring to unprecedented heights.

The growth and potential of the e-commerce industry are nothing short of extraordinary. From small artisanal crafts to multinational corporations, businesses of all sizes now have the ability to showcase their products to a global audience.

The democratization of commerce means that anyone with a unique offering and a strategic approach can carve their niche in this expansive digital marketplace.

Identifying Profitable Niches and Products for Online Retail:

As we navigate the landscape of e-commerce, the question arises.

What makes a successful online store?

The answer lies in understanding the art of niche selection. In a world saturated with choices, finding a specialized corner to occupy can be the key to standing out amidst the digital noise.

This chapter will guide you through the process of identifying profitable niches and products, helping you uncover opportunities that align with both your passions and market demands.

Delving into the intricacies of market research, we will explore how to spot trends, analyze consumer behavior, and pinpoint the sweet spot where your expertise intersects with market needs.

Whether it's the burgeoning world of sustainable products or the evergreen appeal of lifestyle goods, your journey into e-commerce begins with the deliberate choice of a niche that resonates with your vision.

Platforms and Tools:

With a vision in mind and a niche identified, the next step is to choose the right tools to bring your online store to life.

This section of the chapter is a compass through the maze of e-commerce platforms and tools, offering insights into the options available for beginners.

From user-friendly platforms like Shopify and WooCommerce to the more customizable options like Magento, we will explore the features, pros, and cons of each.

This chapter will serve as a roadmap, guiding you through the step-by-step process of setting up your online store, from choosing a domain name to configuring payment gateways.

Step-by-Step Guide to Setting Up an Online Store:

Embark on a hands-on journey as we break down the seemingly complex task of setting up an online store into manageable steps.

From selecting a visually appealing theme to optimizing product listings for search engines, each facet of the process is demystified.

As we navigate the intricacies of e-commerce platforms, you will gain the confidence to customize your storefront, manage inventory, and implement effective marketing strategies.

By the end of this chapter, you'll be equipped not just with knowledge but with a fully functional online store, ready to welcome customers into your digital realm.

The path to e-commerce success begins here—a journey of discovery, strategy, and implementation that transforms your entrepreneurial aspirations into a thriving online business. Let's dive into the world of E-Commerce Empires, where your digital storefront becomes the gateway to untold possibilities.

Embarking on the journey of starting an online business is an exciting venture filled with potential and possibilities. Here are a few key considerations to keep in mind:

Define Your Niche:
Clearly identify your target audience and the unique value proposition you offer. A focused niche allows you to tailor your products or services to meet specific needs.

Build a Strong Online Presence:
Establish a professional and user-friendly website. Leverage social media platforms to connect with your audience and showcase your brand personality.

Prioritize Customer Experience:
Customer satisfaction is paramount. Provide excellent customer service, create an easy

purchasing process, and seek feedback to continually improve.

Master Digital Marketing:
Understand the basics of digital marketing. Utilize social media, content marketing, and search engine optimization to enhance your online visibility.

Invest in Quality Content:
Content is king. Whether through blog posts, videos, or other mediums, create valuable and engaging content that resonates with your target audience.

Secure E-commerce Solutions:
If selling products, choose a secure and user-friendly e-commerce platform. Ensure that payment processing is smooth and secure for customers.

Stay Adaptable:
The online business landscape evolves rapidly. Stay informed about industry trends,

technology advancements, and continuously
adapt your strategies.

Legal and Regulatory Compliance:
Understand the legal and regulatory aspects of
online business, including privacy policies,
terms of service, and compliance with relevant
laws.

Network and Collaborate:
Build relationships with others in your industry.
Networking can open doors to collaborations,
partnerships, and valuable insights.

Track and Analyze Performance:
Utilize analytics tools to track your website's
performance, user behavior, and marketing
efforts. Use data-driven insights to refine your
strategies.

Remember, starting an online business is a
journey, not a destination. Embrace the
learning process, stay resilient in the face of
challenges, and enjoy the fulfillment that
comes with building something of your own.

CHAPTER 2

"Blogging Brilliance Turning Passion into Profit"

In the vast digital landscape, where words are the architects of virtual worlds, blogging stands as a testament to the transformative power of wordsmithery.

This chapter unfolds the narrative of Blogging Brilliance, an exploration into the art of turning passion into profit through the creation of a captivating and sustainable online business.

The Art of Blogging:

At its core, blogging is not just about crafting words into sentences; it's about weaving narratives that resonate, inspire, and engage.

It is the art of storytelling in a digital age, a canvas where passion meets prose, creating a tapestry that draws readers into your world.

The power of blogging lies not only in the stories you tell but in the community you build—a community that shares your passions and finds value in your words.

This section of the chapter dives deep into the essence of blogging, exploring the significance of authentic storytelling and the creation of content that stands out in the crowded online space.

From finding your unique voice to identifying niche markets, we'll navigate the journey of transforming your passion into a blog that captivates and resonates with your audience.

Identifying Niche Markets and Creating Valuable Content:

In the ever-expanding blogosphere, finding your niche is akin to discovering a hidden treasure.

This chapter serves as your treasure map, guiding you through the process of identifying niche markets that align with your passions and expertise. It's not just about finding a topic; it's about finding the intersection of what you love and what your audience craves.

Learn the art of creating valuable content that not only entertains but also informs and enriches the lives of your readers.

We'll explore content creation strategies, from understanding your target audience to mastering the art of headlines and visuals.

By the end of this section, you'll be equipped to build a blog that not only reflects your brilliance but also serves as a valuable resource for your community.

Monetization Strategies:

Passion ignited the flame, but it's sustainable profit that keeps the fire burning.

This chapter delves into the diverse avenues of monetization for bloggers, providing insights into turning your blog into a revenue generating machine.

Exploring Diverse Monetization Avenues for Bloggers:

Uncover the secrets of turning your blog into a business as we explore various monetization avenues.

From traditional advertising to modern methods like affiliate marketing and sponsored content, each path offers unique opportunities for bloggers to earn income.

Tips for Maximizing Revenue Through Advertising, Affiliate Marketing, and Sponsored Content:

Navigate the intricacies of advertising, affiliate marketing, and sponsored content with practical tips and strategies.

Discover how to strike the right balance between monetization and maintaining the authenticity that drew your audience in the first place.

This section provides a roadmap for bloggers to not only monetize effectively but also to build sustainable partnerships that enhance their brand and reader trust.

As we embark on this journey through the realms of Blogging Brilliance, remember.

Your words have the power to not only captivate minds but also to create a livelihood.

The art of blogging is not just about expressing yourself; it's about transforming your passion into a sustainable and lucrative online venture.

Welcome to the world where your brilliance becomes your business.

CHAPTER 3

"Freelance Freedom Monetizing Your Skills"

In the dynamic tapestry of the digital age, the rise of freelancing emerges as a vibrant thread, weaving stories of individuals harnessing their unique skills to craft a career on their terms.

This chapter embarks on a journey into the realm of Freelance Freedom, exploring the avenues through which you can monetize your skills, shape your own destiny, and thrive in the digital marketplace.

Freelancing in the Digital Age:

As traditional employment structures evolve, freelancing has become a cornerstone of the modern workforce.

This section of the chapter illuminates the demand for freelance services in the online marketplace.

The digital age has birthed a global network where businesses, entrepreneurs, and individuals seek specialized skills for projects ranging from graphic design to content creation.

We'll delve into the reasons behind the surge in demand for freelancers, uncovering the advantages this mode of work offers to both clients and freelancers alike.

The flexibility, diversity of projects, and the ability to work with a global clientele make freelancing an enticing avenue for those looking to leverage their skills for financial independence.

Identifying Skills in High Demand and Building a Freelance Business:

Not all skills are created equal in the freelance marketplace.

This section provides guidance on identifying skills in high demand and strategically building a freelance business.

Whether you're a graphic designer, writer, programmer, or possess expertise in a niche field, we'll explore how to assess market needs, position your skills, and create a freelance business that aligns with your passions and financial goals.

Discover the art of diversifying your skill set and adapting to emerging trends to stay relevant in a competitive landscape.

From cultivating your craft to building a portfolio that speaks volumes, this section equips you with the tools needed to transform your skills into a thriving freelance venture.

Freelance Platforms and Marketing:

Freelancing isn't just about having skills—it's about showcasing them to the right audience.

This part of the chapter navigates the landscape of freelance platforms and marketing strategies to help you stand out in the crowded digital marketplace.

Exploring Popular Freelance Platforms and Marketing Strategies:

From Upwork to Fiverr, and beyond, explore the most popular freelance platforms where clients seek skilled professionals.

Understand the nuances of each platform, the types of projects they host, and how to optimize your profile to attract the right clients.

Crafting a Compelling Freelance Profile and Winning Clients:

Your freelance profile is your digital storefront, and this section provides a blueprint for crafting a compelling one.

Learn the art of showcasing your skills, building trust through client testimonials, and presenting yourself as the solution to clients' needs. Navigate the challenges of bidding, setting competitive rates, and delivering exceptional value to clients.

As you embark on the journey of Freelance Freedom, remember that your skills are your currency in this digital marketplace.

This chapter is your guide to navigating the freelancing landscape, transforming your expertise into a sustainable income, and embracing the freedom that comes with being the master of your professional destiny.

Welcome to a world where your skills are not just assets but pathways to success.

CHAPTER 4

"Digital Courses Sharing Knowledge Generating Income"

In the age of digital enlightenment, online learning stands tall as a beacon, drawing learners from every corner of the globe.

This chapter embarks on a journey into the realm of Digital Courses, exploring the landscape where knowledge becomes not just power but also a pathway to income generation.

The Boom of Online Learning:

The chapter unfolds with a gaze upon the flourishing landscape of online learning—a terrain where the quest for knowledge converges with the desire for convenience and accessibility.

The Boom of Online Learning is a testament to the changing dynamics of education, where the traditional classroom is eclipsed by the boundless expanse of the digital realm.

We delve into the factors fueling the popularity of online courses, from the flexibility they offer to the democratization of education.

As we navigate this landscape, consider how your expertise can become a beacon for those seeking to learn and grow in the comfort of their own space.

Identifying Areas of Expertise and Structuring Course Content:

The journey into digital courses begins with a profound self-reflection—an exploration of your areas of expertise and a thoughtful consideration of what knowledge you can impart to others.

This section guides you through the process of identifying your unique strengths, passions, and skills, laying the foundation for crafting valuable course content.

Discover the art of structuring your knowledge in a way that captivates and educates your audience.

From defining learning objectives to creating engaging modules, this section equips you with the tools to transform your expertise into a comprehensive and compelling digital course.

Creating and Marketing Courses:

With the knowledge map in hand, the journey continues into the creation and marketing of your digital courses.

This section explores the platforms that provide a stage for your courses to shine and the strategies to ensure they don't go unnoticed.

Platforms for Hosting and Selling Online Courses:

From industry giants like Udemy and Teachable to more specialized platforms, we'll explore the myriad choices for hosting and selling online courses.

Each platform comes with its unique features, audience, and revenue models. By understanding the landscape, you'll be empowered to choose the platform that aligns with your goals and audience.

Strategies for Effective Course Promotion and Sales:

Creating a course is just the first step; the next is ensuring it reaches the audience hungry for your knowledge.

This section provides insights into effective course promotion and sales strategies. From leveraging social media to employing email marketing tactics, we'll explore avenues to reach potential learners.

Craft a marketing plan that not only attracts students but also builds a community around your courses.

Learn the art of creating compelling course descriptions, utilizing testimonials, and fostering a sense of value that compels learners to invest in their education through your digital offerings.

As you step into the realm of Digital Courses, remember that your knowledge is a gift waiting to be shared.

This chapter is your guide to transforming your expertise into a source of income while contributing to the vast landscape of online learning.

Welcome to a world where your lessons become pathways for others to embark on their learning journeys.

CHAPTER 5

"Affiliate Marketing Mastery Passive Income Potential"

In the labyrinth of online commerce, where connections are currency, Affiliate Marketing emerges as a beacon for those seeking to harness the power of passive income.

This chapter delves into the realm of Affiliate Marketing Mastery, unraveling the intricacies of a model that allows you to monetize without the need for a product of your own.

Affiliate Marketing Basics:

Begin your journey into Affiliate Marketing Mastery with a firm understanding of the basics.

This section unpacks the fundamentals, providing clarity on the dynamics that make affiliate marketing a powerful avenue for generating passive income.

Explore the symbiotic relationship between affiliates, merchants, and consumers.

Grasp the concept of affiliate commissions, referral links, and the role you play as a bridge connecting valuable products or services with a receptive audience.

Identifying Profitable Affiliate Programs and Products:

The success of affiliate marketing hinges on strategic partnerships with the right programs and products.

This section serves as your compass in identifying lucrative opportunities amid the vast sea of affiliate offerings.

Learn to discern between high-quality products and programs that align with your audience's needs.

Uncover the criteria for selecting partners that not only enhance your credibility but also maximize your earning potential.

By the end of this section, you'll be equipped with the knowledge to forge alliances that pave the way for passive income streams.

Effective Marketing Strategies:

Affiliate marketing is not just about embedding links; it's a strategic dance of promotion and persuasion.

This section unveils the effective marketing strategies that elevate your affiliate efforts from transactional to transformative.

Implementing Successful Affiliate Marketing Strategies:

From content integration to email marketing, discover the array of strategies that seamlessly incorporate affiliate links into your digital presence.

This section delves into the art of product reviews, comparison articles, and the strategic placement of affiliate links to optimize conversion rates.

Navigate the ethical considerations of affiliate marketing, ensuring transparency and authenticity in your promotional endeavors.

Understand the importance of building trust with your audience—a trust that becomes the foundation for a sustained and fruitful affiliate marketing journey.

Maximizing Passive Income Through Strategic Promotion:

The true mastery of affiliate marketing lies in the ability to generate passive income—a steady stream that flows without constant intervention.

This section unveils the secrets to maximizing passive income through strategic promotion.

Explore the power of evergreen content, SEO optimization, and the art of creating a funnel that keeps working for you long after the initial promotion.

From leveraging automation tools to understanding the cyclical nature of promotions, this section equips you with the tools to transform your affiliate efforts into a source of consistent and passive income.

As you step into the world of Affiliate Marketing Mastery, remember that your influence is not just a conduit for sales but a catalyst for empowering your audience.

This chapter is your guide to unlocking the potential of passive income through strategic affiliate marketing—a journey where your recommendations become a source of both value and revenue.

Welcome to the realm where your influence transforms into mastery.

Conclusion

"Embarking on Your DIY Online Business Journey"

As we draw the curtain on this comprehensive guide, "Unleashing Wealth"

A DIY Online Business Adventure," take a moment to reflect on the entrepreneurial potential that resides within you.

This journey through the realms of e-commerce, blogging, freelancing, digital courses, and affiliate marketing has been a roadmap—a compass pointing toward the vast landscape of opportunities waiting to be seized.

Reflecting on Entrepreneurial Potential:

In summarizing the top five DIY online businesses and their income potential, we've witnessed the dynamic nature of the digital realm. E-commerce, with its global reach, blogging as a medium of storytelling and community building, freelancing as a gateway to personal and professional freedom, digital courses as vessels of knowledge and income, and affiliate marketing as a path to passive revenue—all these avenues stand as beacons for those ready to embark on their entrepreneurial journey.

Your potential is not confined to the pages of this book but extends to the uncharted territories you choose to explore.

Each of these online business models holds the promise of financial success, and it's your unique blend of passion, skill, and determination that will transform these promises into reality.

Inspiring Confidence in Readers to Pursue Their Entrepreneurial Dreams:

As you close these pages and step into the arena of possibility, carry with you the confidence that success is not a distant destination but a journey of continuous learning and adaptation.

Your dreams are not bound by limitations but fueled by the creativity and resilience that define true entrepreneurs.

This book is not merely a guide; it's an invitation to dream boldly, to embrace uncertainty, and to revel in the joy of creating something uniquely your own.

 Let it be a source of inspiration as you navigate the twists and turns of your entrepreneurial path.

Next Steps:

Now that the groundwork is laid and the possibilities unveiled, your next steps are crucial.

Practical advice is your compass as you set sail into your chosen online business. Whether it's launching your online store, crafting compelling blog posts, bidding on freelancing platforms, creating digital courses, or strategically engaging in affiliate marketing, remember that the journey unfolds one step at a time.

This is not the end; it's a new beginning. Embrace the learning curve, celebrate small victories, and stay resilient in the face of challenges.

Your journey is unique, and the path ahead is yours to shape. Encouraging Ongoing Learning and Adaptation:

In the ever-evolving online landscape, the only constant is change. As you embark on your DIY online business journey, let the spirit of continuous learning be your guide.

Stay abreast of industry trends, embrace emerging technologies, and adapt your strategies as needed. The digital realm rewards those who are nimble, curious, and willing to evolve.

As the final pages turn, the canvas of your online business adventure awaits your brushstroke. May it be a masterpiece—a testament to your creativity, resilience, and entrepreneurial spirit.

This book serves as a comprehensive guide for individuals looking to explore and excel in the world of DIY online businesses.

It covers e-commerce, blogging, freelancing, digital courses, and affiliate marketing, providing insights, strategies, and actionable steps for success in each venture.

May it empower aspiring entrepreneurs to unleash their potential and achieve financial success through online endeavors.

Welcome to the beginning of your DIY online business journey. May it be filled with innovation, fulfillment, and the sweet taste of success. Happy entrepreneuring!

BONUS SECTION

"Mastering Time for Online Business Success"

Welcome to the time management bonus section.

Congratulations on taking the next step towards unlocking the full potential of your online business journey! In this exclusive bonus section, we delve into a crucial aspect often underestimated in the entrepreneurial world — Time Management.

The Precious Currency of Entrepreneurship:

Time, the most invaluable currency at our disposal, plays a pivotal role in shaping the success of your online venture. As you navigate the exciting realm of starting and growing a business in the digital age, mastering the art of time management becomes not just a skill but a cornerstone of your success.

A Brief Overview of the Importance of Time Management for Online Business Success:

In these pages, we will explore the intricate dance between time and productivity, uncovering strategies employed by successful entrepreneurs who have harnessed the power of effective time management to propel their businesses forward.

What to Expect: A Roadmap to Efficiency:

Throughout this bonus section, we will guide you through self-reflection exercises, practical tools for prioritization, and actionable steps to create a daily schedule tailored to your business goals. From effective goal setting to utilizing technology as your ally, we leave no stone unturned in your quest for time mastery.

Why Does Time Management Matter?

Time management is not just about checking off tasks on a to-do list; it's about channeling your efforts strategically to achieve long-term success. The ability to prioritize, plan, and execute tasks efficiently can be the differentiator between a thriving online business and one struggling to gain traction.

So, buckle up for a journey into the heart of effective time management, where each page is a stepping stone towards a more organized, productive, and fulfilling entrepreneurial experience. Let's embark on this transformative exploration together.

To Your Success!

The Time-Productivity Connection:

"Understanding the Relationship Between Effective Time Management and Increased Productivity"

In the dynamic landscape of online entrepreneurship, time isn't just a resource; it's the heartbeat of productivity. On these pages, we delve into the symbiotic relationship between effective time management and the amplification of productivity.

Unlocking the Code: "The Essence of Time Management"

Effective time management isn't merely about squeezing more tasks into your day. It's an art form that involves intentional choices, strategic planning, and a deep understanding of how time influences your overall productivity. As we unravel this connection, you'll gain insights into how optimizing your time can become a catalyst for business growth.

Real-Life Examples of Successful Entrepreneurs:

To illustrate the profound impact of mastering time, we turn to the real stories of successful entrepreneurs who have navigated the challenges of building and scaling online businesses. Their journeys are not just tales of triumph but living proof that deliberate time management is a linchpin for sustainable success.

Meet the Time Masters: "Stories That Inspire"

Discover how entrepreneurs, in diverse industries and niches, attribute a significant part of their achievements to the mastery of their schedules.

From allocating time for innovation to establishing structured routines, these stories offer tangible lessons that you can apply to your own entrepreneurial endeavors.

Beyond the Clock: "Shaping Your Productivity Landscape"

The pages ahead are an exploration of techniques, strategies, and mindsets that bridge the gap between time and productivity.

As you immerse yourself in the narratives of those who have walked this path before, envision how your commitment to effective time management can reshape your own productivity landscape.

Join us on this enlightening journey where the ticking clock becomes your ally, propelling you towards heightened efficiency and, ultimately, the success you envision for your online business.

Assessing Your Time: "A Self-Reflection Tools and Strategies to Evaluate How You Currently Spend Your Time"

Embarking on a journey toward effective time management begins with actively involving you in a process of self-reflection.

In these pages, we provide you with invaluable tools and strategies, acting as your guide in conducting a thorough self-assessment. This empowers you to become your own time detective.

The Time Audit: "Your Personal Time Detective"

Imagine time as currency, and a time audit as your financial statement. We guide you through a step-by-step process of conducting a time audit.

This self-reflection exercise allows you to objectively assess where your time is invested and identify patterns that may be impacting your productivity. Detailed examples and actionable steps ensure you are not just reading but actively participating in this transformative journey.

Identifying Time-Wasting Activities:

Not all activities contribute equally to your entrepreneurial journey. Through relatable examples and guided scenarios, we assist you in identifying time-wasting activities.

This hands-on approach ensures that you can immediately apply your newfound insights to your own circumstances.

Areas for Improvement: "Turning Insights into Action"

Once armed with the knowledge of how you currently spend your time, we transition into a collaborative exploration of areas for improvement.

This isn't about radical shifts but rather subtle adjustments that can lead to significant enhancements in your daily efficiency.

We provide practical frameworks and guide you in prioritizing and optimizing, ensuring that every moment invested contributes meaningfully to your business goals.

Your Time, Your Power: "Taking the Helm of Your Schedule"

These pages are your toolkit for self-discovery and empowerment, and our role is to guide you through each step.

As you engage with the exercises and reflections, remember that this is not just about time; it's about reclaiming control, making intentional choices, and directing your entrepreneurial journey toward success.

Your journey of self-reflection begins here—where time becomes not just a measure but a strategic asset on your path to entrepreneurial mastery.

Prioritizing Tasks The Eisenhower Matrix: "A Practical Tool for Task Prioritization"

Navigating the sea of tasks inherent in the entrepreneurial journey requires not just effort but strategic focus.

In these pages, we introduce you to the Eisenhower Matrix, a practical and powerful tool that acts as your compass in the world of task prioritization.

Understanding the Eisenhower Matrix: " Your Decision-Making Ally"

The Eisenhower Matrix, developed by President Dwight D. Eisenhower, simplifies the complexities of decision-making.

We guide you through the matrix's four quadrants—Urgent and Important, Important but Not Urgent, Urgent but Not Important, and

Neither Urgent nor Important. As your facilitators, we demystify the process, providing real-life examples to illustrate how this matrix can transform your approach to task management.

Differentiating Between Urgent and Important Tasks:

Not all tasks are created equal, and recognizing the distinctions between urgency and importance is fundamental to your efficiency.

As your guides, we share insights into differentiating between urgent and important tasks, ensuring that you can make informed decisions about where to direct your time and energy.

This clarity is the cornerstone of optimal efficiency in your daily endeavors.

Strategies for Effective Prioritization: "Your Roadmap to Success"

Beyond introducing the Eisenhower Matrix, we provide practical strategies to implement this prioritization tool into your daily routine.

Through actionable steps and illustrative scenarios, you'll discover how to seamlessly integrate prioritization into your work flow, enhancing your ability to tackle tasks with purpose and precision.

Your Prioritization Journey: "Guided and Empowered"

Consider these pages as your initiation into the art of task prioritization. Our role is to guide you through the intricacies of the Eisenhower Matrix, empowering you to discern between the urgent and the important.

By the time you turn the page, you'll not only understand the theory but possess the practical tools to prioritize tasks with confidence and clarity.

Your journey to mastering task prioritization begins here—where strategic decisions become the stepping stones to your entrepreneurial success.

Guiding You Toward Prioritization Mastery, Creating a Daily Schedule: "Crafting a Daily Schedule that Aligns with Your Business Goals"

In the dynamic world of entrepreneurship, the daily schedule is your compass, guiding you toward the achievement of your business aspirations.

These pages serve as your workshop for crafting a daily schedule that not only aligns with your goals but becomes the cornerstone of your daily success ritual.

Understanding the Link Between Your Schedule and Business Goals:

Your daily schedule isn't just a series of time slots; it's a strategic roadmap leading you to your entrepreneurial destination.

As your guides, we explore the symbiotic relationship between your daily activities and overarching business goals. We illustrate how intentional scheduling can propel you toward success.

Balancing Work Tasks, Personal Time, and Breaks for Sustained Productivity:

A well-crafted daily schedule is a delicate balance between work, personal time, and rejuvenating breaks.

We provide insights into creating a schedule that prioritizes essential work tasks, nurtures personal well-being, and integrates strategic breaks for sustained productivity.

This holistic approach ensures that your daily routine becomes a source of inspiration and efficiency.

Creating Your Ideal Daily Schedule: "Practical Strategies"

As your companions in this scheduling endeavor, we offer practical strategies for tailoring your daily schedule to your unique needs and business objectives.

From time-blocking techniques to incorporating moments of restorative breaks, these pages provide actionable steps to help you craft a schedule that not only meets the demands of your business but also enhances your overall well-being.

Your Daily Schedule as a Productivity Ally: "A Guided Approach"

Consider these pages your guide in transforming your daily schedule from a mere routine to a powerful ally in your entrepreneurial journey. With each piece of advice and each strategy, you are equipped to not only create but embrace a daily schedule that serves as the scaffolding for your success.

Your journey to crafting a purposeful daily schedule begins here—where each hour becomes an investment in the flourishing future of your business.

Guiding You Toward Daily Schedule: "Master Effective Goal Setting, Setting SMART Goals, Your Blueprint for Success"

In the entrepreneurial landscape, effective goal setting isn't just a skill; it's the compass that directs your efforts toward meaningful accomplishments.

In these pages, we dive into the world of SMART goals—Specific, Measurable, Achievable, Relevant, and Time-bound—an invaluable framework to elevate your goal-setting prowess.

Understanding the SMART Goal Framework: "A Strategic Approach"

The SMART goal framework isn't just an acronym; it's a strategic approach to defining objectives that propel your business forward.

As your guides, we break down each component, offering practical insights and relatable examples that demystify the process of setting goals that are not only inspiring but also attainable.

Breaking Down Long-Term Goals into Manageable Tasks:

Long-term goals are the stars on your entrepreneurial horizon, but reaching them requires navigating a series of manageable tasks.

We guide you through the art of breaking down formidable long-term goals into smaller, achievable tasks. By the end of these pages, you'll possess the tools to turn lofty aspirations into actionable steps.

From Vision to Execution: "Your Goal-Setting Journey"

Setting goals is not just about vision; it's about execution. These pages provide a roadmap for translating your entrepreneurial vision into a series of tangible and realistic objectives.

By embracing the principles of SMART goal setting and task breakdown, you'll be empowered to steer your business toward success with purpose and precision.

Your SMART Goal Setting Expedition: "A Guided Adventure"

Consider these pages your guidebook for an expedition into the realm of effective goal setting.

As you immerse yourself in the principles of SMART goals and task breakdown, you're not just learning; you're actively participating in the transformative process of turning aspirations into achievements.

Your journey to effective goal setting begins here—where each goal becomes a stepping stone to the thriving future of your business.

Guiding You Toward Goal Setting Mastery: "Tools and Apps for Time Management Overview of Popular Time Management Tools and Applications"

In the fast-paced world of entrepreneurship, technology can be your greatest ally in mastering time management.

In these pages, we embark on a journey through a curated selection of popular time management tools and applications.

This overview serves as your gateway to a more organized and efficient business life.

Navigating the Tech Landscape: "Your Introduction to Time Management Apps"

With a multitude of options available, choosing the right time management tools can be overwhelming.

As your navigators, we provide a comprehensive overview of tools designed to enhance your productivity.

From task organizers to collaborative platforms, we highlight each tool's unique features, ensuring you can make informed decisions that align with your specific needs.

Practical Tips on Integrating Technology to Streamline Your Workflow:

Integrating technology into your daily routine isn't just about the tools; it's about creating a seamless workflow.

We offer practical tips on incorporating these time management apps into your routine, ensuring that technology becomes an enabler, not a hindrance. Whether you're a tech enthusiast or a beginner, these pages empower you to harness the full potential of these tools.

Your Tech Toolbox: "A Guided Tour"

Consider these pages your guided tour through the tech toolbox of time management. From calendar applications to task trackers, each recommendation is presented with insights into its functionalities and real-world applications.

By the time you conclude this section, you'll not only be familiar with these tools but equipped to elevate your efficiency through the strategic integration of technology.

From Tools to Transformation: "Your Tech-Infused Productivity Journey"

As you explore the world of time management tools, envision not just a collection of apps but a transformative journey toward a more streamlined and efficient workflow. Your business deserves the best, and these pages guide you toward embracing technology as a strategic partner in your pursuit of entrepreneurial success.

The Power of Saying No: "The Art of Setting Boundaries and Managing Commitments"

In the tapestry of entrepreneurship, the ability to say "no" is a brushstroke that defines the contours of your success.

These pages unravel the art of setting boundaries and managing commitments—a crucial skill that empowers you to navigate the delicate balance between ambition and overwhelm.

Understanding the Art of Saying No: "Strategic Approach"

Saying "no" isn't a rejection; it's a strategic choice that preserves your focus and energy.

We guide you through the nuances of this art, providing insights into the importance of setting boundaries.

Learn how to discern between opportunities that align with your goals and those that may derail your progress.

The Liberating Impact of Saying "No" to Non-Essential Tasks:

Your time is a finite resource, and every "yes" is a commitment of that resource.

We explore the liberating impact of saying "no" to non-essential tasks, revealing how this seemingly small word can be a catalyst for greater productivity and fulfillment.

These pages offer practical scenarios and tips to empower you in gracefully declining commitments that do not align with your vision.

Balancing Generosity and Prioritization: "Your Guide to Empowered Decision-Making"

Saying "no" isn't about shutting doors; it's about selectively choosing the doors that lead to your desired destination. We provide a guide to balanced decision-making, where the power of saying "no" becomes a tool for empowerment rather than limitation. By the end of these pages, you'll appreciate the strategic art of decline as a key component of your entrepreneurial toolkit.

Your Empowered Journey: "Saying "No" with Purpose"

Consider these pages your guide in wielding the power of saying "no" with purpose. As you embrace the art of setting boundaries, envision not restriction but liberation—liberation from the unnecessary, from overwhelm, and from dilution of your focus. Saying "no" becomes a declaration of your commitment to your vision and the intentional pursuit of your entrepreneurial dreams.

"Summing Up the Importance of Effective Time Management"

As we reach the culmination of this journey into the realms of time management for online business success, it's crucial to reflect on the profound significance of the strategies and insights shared within these pages.

Effective time management is not just a skill; it's the heartbeat of entrepreneurial success.

Throughout this exploration, we've uncovered the intricacies of self-reflection, task prioritization, daily scheduling, goal setting, and the strategic use of technology.

Each facet contributes to a harmonious symphony of efficiency, guiding you toward a future where your online business thrives and flourishes.

Encouragement and Motivation for Readers:

To every reader who has embarked on this transformative exploration, take a moment to acknowledge the commitment you've made to your own success.

The journey of effective time management is not without its challenges, but within those challenges lie opportunities for growth, resilience, and triumph.

As you integrate these strategies into your entrepreneurial routine, remember that success is not solely measured by outcomes but by the journey itself.

Embrace each step, celebrate small victories, and view setbacks as stepping stones toward greater achievements.

Your commitment to effective time management is an investment in the sustainability and prosperity of your online business.

Implementing Strategies for Success: "A Call to Action"

Now, armed with a toolkit of strategies and insights, the next step is implementation. The power of these pages lies not just in the knowledge they impart but in the actions you take based on that knowledge. Take ownership of your time, prioritize with purpose, and let every decision be a conscious step toward your vision.

A Grateful Farewell:

As your guides in this exploration, we extend our deepest gratitude for entrusting us with a part of your entrepreneurial journey.

May the wisdom gained within these pages propel you to new heights, and may the symphony of effective time management resonate throughout the chapters of your online business story.

To Your Success and Beyond!

BEYOND DESIRES

"Blogger Emma Venture"

In the dim glow of her computer screen, Emma Venture nervously contemplated the next chapter of her online journey.

After much contemplation and a fair share of self-reflection, she had decided to embrace her passion and launch a blog that delved into the world of fetishes.

Little did she know that this endeavor would not only challenge societal norms but also confront her own deeply held secret.

Starting "Beyond Desires" was no easy feat for Emma. She grappled with the fear of judgment, wondering if the world was ready to accept the unfiltered truth about desires that lingered beneath the surface.

The initial struggle was not just about setting up a blog—it was about exposing a part of herself she had kept hidden for far too long.

Emma's personal journey with fetishes, specifically her own fascination with feet, added an unexpected layer of complexity. As she crafted the first few posts, she shared the struggles she faced in embracing this aspect of herself.

The fear of being labeled, the worry about how friends and family would react, and the internal battles that ensued—Emma poured it all into her writing.

The spicy twist in her narrative lay in the raw honesty with which she unveiled her own story. The blog became a canvas for her personal triumphs and tribulations, offering readers an intimate glimpse into the struggles of self-acceptance. Emma's vulnerability became the very essence of "Beyond Desires."

The response from her audience was mixed but surprisingly supportive. Readers from around the world began to share their own stories, finding solace in Emma's authenticity.

The comment section became a virtual confessional, where individuals felt liberated to acknowledge and explore their own desires.

As the blog gained momentum, Emma's confidence soared. The spicy allure of "Beyond Desires" wasn't just in its content but in the courage it took to lay bare one's vulnerabilities.

Emma's personal triumph emerged not only in the success of her blog but in her newfound acceptance of herself.

And so, Emma Venture, the once-reluctant blogger, became a beacon of authenticity in a world that often thrived on facades.

"Beyond Desires" wasn't just a blog—it was a testament to the power of embracing one's true self, even when that self carried unconventional passions.

In the end, Emma's spicy story became a celebration of self-discovery, acceptance, and the transformative journey that occurs when one has the courage to venture beyond societal expectations.

Dear Imaginative Souls

As we delve into the captivating narrative of "Beyond Desires," I want to remind you that this story is a fictional tapestry woven with threads of inspiration. Emma Venture, the intrepid blogger, is a figment of imagination created to ignite sparks of possibility.

While the tale of "Beyond Desires" is a testament to the transformative power of embracing authenticity, please tread with caution in the real world. Starting a blog, especially on unconventional topics, demands careful consideration of personal boundaries, privacy, and the potential impact on your life.

Real-life journeys may involve complexities and challenges that surpass the boundaries of our fictional realm. If you're contemplating a similar venture, take the time to evaluate the potential consequences, both personal and professional. Seek guidance from mentors, consider the legal implications, and prioritize your well-being.

Remember, the world of blogging is vast and diverse, offering countless opportunities to share your authentic voice without delving into overly sensitive or controversial territories. Authenticity doesn't always demand the disclosure of deeply personal details.

So, as you embark on your own creative endeavors, let "Beyond Desires" serve as a spark of inspiration, a beacon reminding you of the incredible possibilities that storytelling can unfold. May your real-life adventures be filled with wisdom, prudence, and the joy of self-expression.

Wishing you imaginative journeys and thoughtful reflections.

About the Authors

Meet the dynamic duo behind the inspiring guide "DO IT YOURSELF ONLINE VENTURE: Unleashing the potential of the top five profitable online businesses," featuring a bonus section on time management—Penelope Killarney Americus and Jolanta Blue Polishky.

Penelope Killarney Americus:

Penelope is a seasoned individual with roots in the USA, where she was born, and a heart molded in the diverse landscapes of Canada, where she was raised. Over the years, Penelope has accumulated a wealth of experience and wisdom, showcasing that age is no barrier to pursuing one's dreams. Her journey has been marked by resilience and a relentless pursuit of passion. Before venturing into the world of online business, Penelope served as a Director of Active Living, embodying her commitment to a healthy and fulfilling lifestyle. Today, she stands as an example that it is never too late to embark on a

new adventure and embrace the
entrepreneurial spirit.

Jolanta Blue Polishky:

Hailing from Poland, Jolanta Blue Polishky's
life took a transformative turn when she
relocated to Canada. A mechanical engineer by
profession, Jolanta's story is one of
adaptability and determination. Meeting
Penelope at a previous work site sparked a
connection that would lead them to venture
into uncharted territories together. Jolanta's
technical expertise combined with her passion
for writing and service laid the foundation for
their collaborative effort. Despite being well
into her years, Jolanta is a living testament to
the belief that age is no barrier to innovation
and reinvention.

Together:

Penelope and Jolanta, an unlikely yet complementary pair, decided to forge their own path and explore the world of online entrepreneurship. Their shared love for writing and the desire to empower others led to the creation of "DO IT YOURSELF ONLINE VENTURE." The book not only unlocks the secrets of profitable online businesses but also reflects their commitment to encouraging others to pursue their dreams, regardless of age or background.

As authors, Penelope Killarney Americus and Jolanta Blue Polishky bring a unique blend of experience, passion, and a shared belief in the transformative power of starting anew. Through their words and insights, they inspire readers to embrace change, unleash their potential, and prove that it's never too late to embark on a journey of self-discovery and entrepreneurial success.

"In the dynamic landscape of online entrepreneurship, authenticity is your greatest asset. Embrace the uniqueness of your journey, for it is the authenticity of your story that will resonate with others. In the words of Seth Godin, 'The cost of being wrong is less than the cost of doing nothing.' Don't fear mistakes; embrace them as stepping stones toward growth. Tim Ferriss reminds us, 'What we fear doing most is usually what we most need to do.'

Remember, perfection is not the goal; progress is. As Sheryl Sandberg wisely puts it, 'Done is better than perfect.' Gary Vaynerchuk advocates understanding your personal DNA, emphasizing that your authenticity is your superpower. 'You have to understand your own personal brand and stay true to it.'

Elon Musk's bold declaration, 'Failure is an option here. If things are not failing, you are not innovating enough,' underscores the importance of taking calculated risks.

As you navigate the entrepreneurial journey, heed the advice of Peter Thiel: 'Competition is for losers.' Instead, strive to create a unique value proposition. Chris Guillebeau encourages you to align your life with your passion: 'The most important thing is to find what you were put on this Earth to do and align your life accordingly.'

Simon Sinek's timeless wisdom, 'People don't buy what you do; they buy why you do it,' underscores the significance of communicating your purpose. Finally, from J.K. Rowling: 'It is impossible to live without failing at something unless you live so cautiously that you might as well not have lived at all.'

In this digital realm, be true to yourself, embrace your journey, and let your authenticity shine. Your story, with all its twists and turns, is the key to connecting with others and leaving an indelible mark on the entrepreneurial landscape."